Praise for Something Beautiful, Something Good:

"Something Beautiful, Something Good is a touching and poignant story. It is so clear Pamela has been hand-picked by God to share a hopeful redemption story. A three time incarcerated woman, Pamela Gillins, found freedom in Christ. When we ask, God delivers us from all of our messes, those we create and those we are subjected to by others. "

-JENNIFER WEISS,
Author of Holy Spirit Adventures

"A true prison success story! Pamela reached out to Jesus, and he heard her cry. Those with his heart of kindness and empathy trained her, while in prison, on a career path and helped her get a degree. This story carries so much hope."

- TONI RILEY,
Author of The Bright Side of Broken

DOVE

PUBLISHING HOUSE

Dedication

I dedicate this book to my parents,
Norris and Etta Gillins.

Thank you for teaching me to love and care for
others. I'm truly grateful that I was introduced to
God in my home. The trust I had as a child of being
safe and secure has allowed me to have the same
confidence and security in Jesus Christ. Thanks,
Daddy and Mommy.

Contents

Part I: The Caterpillar

Part II: The Cocoon

Part III: The Butterfly

Prologue

At the age of two or three, I remember seeing a man on a tractor clearing. The man's skin was very pale, not like my dark skin. This was my first time seeing a 'White man.'

I remember waking every morning to watch the White man on the tractor. I don't remember exactly what I was thinking at the time, but I don't recall envying his pale skin. I attended kindergarten, and everyone's skin was dark, and I don't remember feeling out of place or uncomfortable. However, after a few years passed and I started elementary school, I became embarrassed by the darkness of my skin. Whenever my mother, a beautiful Black woman, would come to my school for any reason, l felt ashamed because of the hue of our skin. I can't remember whether being aware of the difference in skin colors mattered when I started school or whether it happened gradually. Why? What made me feel this way? I became withdrawn and quiet around people I didn't know, fearing their thoughts of me.

My childhood in our home was the best, or so I thought. My mother was a housewife, with five children between herself and my father. I had two older sisters from my mother's first marriage. Cynthia and Shirley were already out of the house and married with children. Mother was constantly supportive, and we had everything we needed.

However, my mother soon became ill after the birth of my sister, Nora. Mother was forty years old, and her illness returned each year at different times. After several years of ups and downs, she succumbed to her illness. One month before her death, I turned eighteen years old and gave birth to my first child ten days later.

My daughter was only three weeks old at the time of my mother's passing, and I was left to assume the responsibility of caring for and performing the necessary maternal duties for our family. I tried my best to fill the role required, but I was distracted and pulled in different directions into areas of life I had no previous knowledge of.

To understand my story, you must grasp the turbulent scene surrounding me. From 1961-1968 our schools and communities were segregated. The only places that I recall our family visiting were church and school. Everyone's skin color was different shades of the same brown, and this was my normal.

From December 1979 through the 1990s, major events occurred in Miami-Dade County, specifically in Liberty City. This is where I ended up as I attempted to find my way in this life as an adult.

First, on December 17, 1979, Arthur McDuffie was beaten to death after being involved in a high-speed police chase. Then in May of 1980, the White officers were acquitted on all charges, which incited a race riot. The city was in an uproar, and local businesses were burned to the ground. During the turmoil, Yahweh Ben Yahweh moved in with a religious cult that brought fear, intimidation and murder to the community. This came about because this religious group began purchasing several apartment buildings and began the eviction of many residents. We all tried to steer clear of this cultish group, but families were forced to find other places to live with no funds to relocate.

Emerging from the riots and chaos was a group of people the Miami detectives dubbed the "Opa Locka 200" check cashing ring. An estimated 200 people were affiliated with the check cashing ring. I landed amid this fast-moving, dramatic, and not to mention dangerous money-making venture. Most of the checks being cashed were from the local businesses that burned down in the riots.

My seven-year affiliation with the Opa Locka check-cashing gang resulted in multiple incarcerations. These events contributed to my involvement in, and proximity to, situations I had only seen on television.

I was one of the people who survived and will share my story and give God the glory. God, in His mercy, has restored many lives and convinced many souls, including me, that even in the worst of times, He alone can save and give many another day to reflect on His goodness and grace.

Now, I have been changed.

Please go the distance with me, knowing that you or someone you know is worth saving. God is the same yesterday, today, and forever. He is still transforming lives into true worshippers and witnesses of His amazing love, forgiveness, and reconciliation through Jesus Christ. He can still make something beautiful and something good out of your life.

PREFACE

My God Visions

As I laid down to sleep, I began to dream. I walked with many people around me at a church or family gathering. We were in a park, and a pastor I knew (who recently died) threw a t-shirt to me. It was gold with red writing. The pastor owned a novelty shop, with shirts, African attire, and artifacts sold in his store.

After getting the t-shirt, I walked over to where his wife was sitting, and we both read what was printed on the front of the shirt. The word BABY was across the top with three bold arrows pointing down.

Her words to me were, "Do what you must do."

It was 2004. When I woke up from the dream, I felt what I saw was special, but I didn't know the meaning or origin. I just continued to pray and I waited.

Some days later, as I slept, I had another dream. This time I was pregnant, and in my old bedroom of the house I grew up in. I looked out of the window, and three men were sitting in chairs facing the window, watching me.

I walked over and closed the blinds, then, immediately, one of the men came up to the window and snatched the blinds open. The look on his face said to me, "I'm watching you."

This time I was convinced that something spiritual was speaking to me. So I prayed and asked the Lord what this all meant, which led me to the third dream that persuaded me this message was indeed from God.

This time in my dream, I stood on a sidewalk. I saw a car coming and noticed a little child in the street that was about to be hit by the vehicle. I couldn't stand to see the baby injured, so I woke up.

As I sat in prayer, I recognized that God presented the first dream or vision; the last ones were from my enemy.

A couple of years passed, then I had the fourth dream of a baby. I had this big, beautiful baby in my arms that I was taking to give back to a family. I walked up three stairs and then knocked on a door. As I entered, I laid the child on the counter and sat on the couch, waiting for someone to take the baby I was returning. People in the home walked back and forth, ignoring the child. I turned to look and saw that the baby had something in his mouth.

I ran over, took the object out, and decided I needed to leave. As I walked back down the three steps, I noticed there was now no gate by which to exit. I ran from one end of the fence to the other, trying very hard to leave.

Then I woke up.

These dreams instilled in me the belief that God has chosen me for this project. My life's testimony will open up dialogue in hopes of bringing deliverance and freedom to traumatized souls so that healing will come. I don't believe that I alone have gone through and experienced many of the types of situations discussed in this book. Prayerfully, just believe God and Solomon, "There's nothing new under the sun."

In 2013, while recovering from surgery, God's purpose was made clear. At that time, I started to do what I believed He wanted me to do. Write this book.

The many trials I've encountered assured me that I must complete my story and send a message of hope. God already knows everything about His children and their needs. The Lord desires to deliver us from the guilt and shame of our past. While reading God's Word one morning, the Lord spoke clearly to me. He stated that my past was in my future. God was with us during the storms of life, and He never left us. How we processed what we went through caused our pain and set us up for failure, NOT GOD!

Now that we have come into the knowledge of His Son, our Savior, we WIN! We have been preserved for just such a time as this. Our Father saved us on purpose and for His purpose. Many have seen the change in me and now desire to know the Savior in their hearts. God is no respecter of person. What He has done for me, He will do the same for you. Amen.

Thank you once again for making room for me to share. God bless.

PART I
The Caterpillar

CHAPTER 1

The Beginning

My story is that of a young girl with great responsibility placed upon her very early in life.

As a toddler, I remember looking out the window of our old wooden frame house, watching a White man on a big, yellow tractor. He was clearing the land of trees and bushes. Later I realized that my parents were having a house built there, which would be the place I would call home for the next fifteen years.

My father was a very hard-working man. All he wanted my mother to do was to raise and care for his children. He traveled from Baltimore, Maryland, where he worked as a chauffeur, to Miami, where he started a lawn service that afforded him the resources to care for his household successfully.

When I started kindergarten, I remember this lady and her mother would load us all, maybe 10 to 12 children, into her station wagon and then take us to her home in Ojus, Florida. This was a community in Miami, Florida, where she taught us to read and write. I believe that Ms. Forbes was her name and that this lady made more than one trip to get the children to her home. Only now do I realize how many people sacrificed for us to be educated. A designated school building did come, but it was not until a few years later that my sister began kindergarten.

On Sundays, the children went to church after completing Sunday school. There were five of us, two older boys and three girls. My mother always came later. She would prepare dinner before she left home and then join us at church. In those days, my dad never attended church. I believe that was his special time of rest after a busy week. The three girls sang with the youth choir, but I don't remember my brothers participating in any activities there. Mother was the financial secretary for the church and took great pleasure in serving in God's house.

During these times, life was great. Even though I didn't really understand much of what the pastor taught, I felt that Sundays were special. After coming home, we all would unwind while Mother prepared and warmed our dinner. We all sat down to eat at the same time, the children in the kitchen and my parents in the dining room.

During the days, my mother would play gospel music all day in our home, and the atmosphere was always peaceful and serene. Each week, every day, one of the girls would clean the dishes and kitchen, and everything needed to be cleaned; the cabinets, walls, and fridge. Finally, the last thing to do was empty the garbage and mop the floor. Only then was the chore for that day completed. The girls each had a week for whatever chore my mother assigned to us.

This was one of many chores around our house. I never had the option of exchanging or paying someone else to do what was expected of me.

Mother had a list of chores for each of us to complete once we were out of school. Nothing could happen or be discussed until after these were completed. She taught us to iron clothes by sprinkling water to get the wrinkles out. My sisters and I learned how to separate laundry and cook. Afterward, we could ask to go outside to play or do whatever we wanted.

At six years old, I remember having significant responsibility for my two sisters, Ruby and Nora. As I walked to first grade, I walked my sister Ruby to kindergarten across the street each morning. One day I was in a hurry to get to my class, so I asked my sister to cross the street alone. I assured her that she would be just fine.

Within moments of sitting in my assigned seat, Ruby was standing in the doorway of my classroom, screaming, "I want my sister to take me to school."

She caused such a commotion that my teacher asked me to please take her across the street. Needless to say, I never tried to dodge my responsibility like that again.

Nora, on the other hand, would rock and bump her head against the pillow to go to sleep at night. This was annoying, but just as Ruby did, she felt secure being with her big sister. I would tell her that a monster was watching from the window and that if she didn't stop bumping her head, I would allow it to come in and take her away. After Nora begged and pleaded, I would tell the monster under my command to go away, giving her another chance.

Where was my security?

CHAPTER 2

The Heavy Burden of Shame

My father's cousin, who we called "Uncle Sonny," terrified me. He always dressed nice, smelled good, and wore lots of jewelry, but he was an alcoholic.

As soon as he entered our home, he would ask for me. "Where is Trish?" That was my nickname.

He would sit me on his lap, touch me, and squeeze me in places that made me uncomfortable. I didn't know if what I was experiencing was right or wrong, but I hated to see him coming. When I became a little older, I would hide under the bed as soon as I saw his big, shiny car pull up in our driveway.

I never understood why no one questioned my reasons for hiding. Everyone knew that I was bashful, and now as I think about things, I believe that my reaction to people was one of shame. I was ashamed of many thoughts I had and disobedient things I'd done that no one knew about but me. I didn't want to say anything that would cause problems. I also felt it would all go away if I didn't say anything about Uncle Sonny.

Another reason was that I didn't know what to say. Topics such as incest, rape, and inappropriate sexual behavior were not discussed in the presence of children.

I asked myself, "Is this wrong?"

All I knew was that I did not like what was happening to me. I don't remember anything serious happening to me with my Uncle Sonny, but I began to shy away and withdraw more. I felt guilty. Of what? I did not know. I would be asked, "What's wrong?" I rarely responded but just remained silent. My mother noticed the change in me and decided that all of her girls must participate in ministry while at church.

This is the way she put it. "You will no longer be just a floor member in the church." The panic of being in front of people to sing and participate in church programs was terrifying.

When I was eight years old, my mother became sick with an illness recurring yearly. I did all the cooking, cleaning, washing dishes and clothes, dressing both sisters for school, combing their hair, and preparing my dad's breakfast before he went to work.

As I think back, the chores were many, but everything came naturally. I pushed myself every day to get everything done. I knew my mother depended on me, and I didn't want to disappoint her.

As I lay in my bed at night, I thought over everything I needed to do as soon as I awoke the next morning. After all, I believed everything that needed to be done was my responsibility.

When my mother was ill and in the hospital or recovering at home, I ran all of the household activities like a well-oiled machine. I remember hearing my aunt say to someone that our home looked like Etta, my mother, was there. As a result of receiving all this praise, I began to manipulate situations to work in my favor. Oh yes, in their eyes, I could do no wrong.

I began to feel very good about being depended upon and meeting everyone's expectations. I loved the praise and worked extremely hard to get every kind word.

So, what happened?

CHAPTER 3

Changing

After a few years, their expectations meant less and less to me. I began to realize that I had no dreams or expectations for myself. I only woke up to deal with the matters at hand for a very long time. I knew exactly what to do when a problem arose to avoid disturbing or disrupting our normal routine.

But my mind was so consumed by the duties that I found it harder to concentrate in class at school. The thoughts of chores that needed my attention monopolized my thoughts. Yes, I'm almost sure that this is where I began to lose interest in school. I found that it was difficult to keep up. I started to drift. I pulled away from all my childhood friends and found a new set of folks to hang around with in my little free time.

The schools were segregated until 1968-1969, meaning people of color attended schools in their community while Whites attended theirs. But societal pressures increased as the times began to change. Our district implemented what was termed as 'star-bursting.' Star-bursting is the term used to describe what was taking place when Black children were bussed to other White schools for integration.

We were so excited, at first, about being bused to schools north and south of our communities. Integration was happening.

As we exited the bus and began walking down the hall towards the main auditorium, where we would receive orientation and schedules, I noticed a commotion between some Black and White students. I didn't know whether this was a protest or whether children of color were being targeted. Sadly, I must admit I joined in the brawl.

I never found out the cause of what occurred, and afterward, I don't believe I ever connected with the school system again. I felt ashamed for my behavior, and the look in the teachers' and students' eyes created a terrible environment for me. The spirit of fear was in the expressions of some students as if they were just waiting for the next violent event. My focus turned solely toward the chores that I had at home.

The fact that I had joined in hurting people for no apparent reason scarred me. In fact, even fifty years later, I find myself being too tolerant of allowing people to put me in abusive situations or treat me poorly. Yes, I tend to give everyone the benefit of the doubt. So much healing is needed, and I now realize the trauma and agony I've suppressed. Regretfully I have absolutely no memory of any teacher, class friend, or other activity I may have participated in that school year. Lost? Yes!

Our neighborhoods were also rapidly becoming infected with drugs and diseases at the time. Needless to say, a lot was going on outside and inside our homes. I don't remember any adult taking the time to explain what was happening and, more importantly, what was expected of us. As I think back, I wonder whether our parents knew or had any idea what was going on or how this transition would affect the children. I believe this only increased my disconnect from school.

I remember going to classes, hating that my skin was so dark. It never mattered that everyone always told me how pretty I was. I was afraid of being out front and in the light, so I maneuvered in darkness. I did most of my personal fun things that mattered to me alone. The shame of how God had made me caused me to feel less than everyone else. This mindset began developing around age six or seven and grew to become a part of me.

What happened? What had I been exposed to that caused me to sink into such a terrible place?

Where had I engaged with such demoralizing demons that obviously drained me of most of my self-esteem?

How could I, a child, be embarrassed by the darkness of my beautiful Black mother's skin when she came to my school for any reason?

In Psalm 139:1, 13-14 (NIV), the Bible says, "O LORD, you have searched me and you know me. For you created my inmost being; you knit me together in my mother's womb. I praise you because I am fearfully and wonderfully made; your works are wonderful, I know that full well."

These verses speak of a God who knows us. The words tell me that my Lord was there and that He put me together beautifully in my mother's womb. At this time, I had never heard this Psalm or read it.

How did my mind get so twisted? Inside I was screaming, "HELP!" I never understood why but even then, I knew my thoughts were taking me to a place against my will, and I had absolutely no power to stop them.

CHAPTER 4

Fitting In

Beyond my issues with school in general, at thirteen, I began to get very familiar with boys. I would feel strange things going on in my body. I remember going to the movies on Saturdays. It only cost 25 cents if you cut the coupon out of the Sun Tattler newspaper on Tuesday every week. There, we would meet boys and kiss and touch each other. There was not much for children to do other than hang out at the parks. As it is still today, we were told that only the bad kids hung out at the park.

I did join the softball team coached by my American History teacher. Several of my classmates also played. It was fun, and I think we played for two or three summers. But as we got older, no one wanted to play in the dirt anymore.

My mother would still get sick for a few months every year and be hospitalized for a week or two. During these times, I learned how to maneuver all things to accomplish everything I wanted to do, and nothing was lacking. I felt like I was different at school from who I was at home.

Was I living a double life? No, I was trained to serve and be what everyone else needed me to be at that moment.

My mother began spending a lot of time with me when she felt better. She bought a sewing machine, patterns, and pretty materials for me. I would sew every afternoon when I came home from school after chores. I enjoyed making shorts and tops for my little sister, Ruby, and me.

I didn't know at the time that Mother was searching for something that would pique my interest and pull me away from those "friends." I remember once she and I went to a Muslim Mosque. We watched films explaining their faith and beliefs. Mother didn't drive, and l remember the very long bus ride from one county to the next.

There must have been a purpose for these trips because I had two sisters, but I was the only focus. And my trips didn't stop there. I also went to hear prophets and preachers.

The pastor that I will never forget is Reverend Ike. After leaving this service, I woke up with red prayer cloths on my bed and his pamphlets, maybe twenty, under my mattress. I never questioned any of what was occurring. I just wanted to silence the shame inside of me and to be blessed somehow.

The next few years were a blur to me. Our family was still attending church regularly, and when Mother was able, she joined us. I've been trying to make sense of the pastor's message for a long time. Even though he offered encouraging words, I'd never felt God's promises or blessings included me. With all that was going on inside and outside of me, I just didn't believe I was one of the people who should or could benefit from what the Lord offered.

The way I heard and understood the message implied that my life needed to line up with God's requirements first. Only then would I qualify and be allowed to participate in the goodness given. Whether the enemy blocked my hearing or I just misunderstood, repentance never entered my consciousness. Sadly, I had no connection with the power behind the words.

CHAPTER 5

Loss

When I was seventeen, I got pregnant and moved in with my boyfriend, Alfred. On August 25, 1975, my daughter was born. One day my mother sent my dad to tell me to come home and that Alfred should also come. Knowing my father and the fact that he never once looked at me while he spoke to me made me afraid. Of what? I wasn't sure, but I knew I needed to go home.

I was not prepared for the chain of events waiting for me. Mother's pain from how the illness was deteriorating her body and the crying, moaning, and distress penetrated my soul. My dad asked me to come home to help with my mother's illness.

One day I remember praying, asking God to take her out of her misery. Yes, I believe I said, "Let her die." I only wanted her free from her constant suffering, or so I thought. I thought that if I didn't have to watch her in agony, maybe some of the torment within me would dispel. This was the very first prayer that I prayed and received an answer to.

Three weeks after the birth of my child, my mother passed away. Upon hearing of Mother's death, something inside told me that all of her sighs and moans had been for me and the rest of her loved ones she would soon leave. Mother knew for a long time that I was in a bad place, and none of her efforts seemed to help me.

A tremendous wave of guilt came upon me. I was ashamed of how I disappointed her; now, I'd destroyed our entire family with my prayer. I wanted Mother to be released, but now I realize we all felt the void and consequences of her being gone from each of our lives. I felt this heavy burden of guilt watching my dad suffer without her. It was too much. I needed to make sure all the bills were paid, dinner cooked, clothes cleaned, and make sure that upon my father's arrival home from work, he met a quiet atmosphere around the house

I didn't really know anything about life or motherhood. I knew how to be a helpful sister and obedient daughter for my dad but not a mom! I felt completely lost.

At the funeral service, the casket opened, and I was carried out. I couldn't bear to say goodbye. My heart was exploding inside my chest, each beat saying, *I can't go back, I can't say I'm sorry, Mother, I can't ...*

The one person I knew loved me unconditionally was gone forever.

Now, there would be no one to hold me at night when I was afraid of the peeping Tom, the one my mother and I saw at our bathroom window! My only source of comfort was gone forever.

Eventually, this loss became so overwhelming that I felt it necessary to get as far away from this reality as possible. I just started running. Where? I didn't have any clue. My search for love to fill the emptiness made me an easy target to be used and abused. One day I realized that all my energy was futile because guilt and shame were everywhere I went. It took me twelve years and three prison terms to experience true freedom of Spirit.

CHAPTER 6

My Mother's Shoes

It was rough trying to fill my mother's shoes around the house. My younger sisters, Nora and Ruby, were very disobedient, and my dad had a different woman each month. I supposed he was filling his own needs in his life.

To cope, I started using drugs, Mary J and pills. Alfred, my baby's father, worked and made decent money, I think. I will put it this way: we could purchase everything for the baby, buy a few groceries and then get high the entire weekend. Week after week, the same routine.

Oh, how I wished I had gone to New York with my cousin, Flora. Years ago, my mother discussed and made plans with Flora, but no one told me until it was too late. Late, meaning my dad refused to let me go, fearing people would think he couldn't care for his own children. (A man thing!)

Things around my house were crazy. My brothers, Nathaniel and Michael, were both in prison. My oldest brother, Nathaniel, was in a corner store while it was being robbed, along with two other friends. They were all made to lie on the floor with their eyes closed. There were two White ladies in the store as well. Nathaniel was accused of the robbery, and neither of the other guys were with him. At the time, Nathaniel was only sixteen. My dad sold his property to pay a White lawyer, and as you know, Nathaniel was found guilty. Afterward, Nathaniel said there was no God because if there were, he would not have gone to prison for something he did not do. Nathaniel was destroyed emotionally. There was only one winner in the trial, the White lawyer.

My dad wanted to get married, move in with his woman then rent out our home. Yes, we all had to move out. And guess what? I was pregnant again. It had been three years since my mother's passing, and my life had gone nowhere.

Each day was extremely challenging beyond anything I could have imagined. Our home went from an organized operation to total chaos.

Alfred let someone use his car, the individual stole hubcaps, and the police said, "Snitch or go to a drug program." Alfred chose the program.

No one knew I was pregnant, but I couldn't repeat what I did last year. Let me explain. On January 8, 1977, I left home, as usual, to pay bills or something of that nature, only to stop first to have an abortion before it was too late. I had birth control pills, but the pills seemed to make me gain unwanted weight.

Six months later, on June 25, 1977, I was back at the clinic for another abortion. I felt terrible but knew I couldn't handle being pregnant and on drugs. It never occurred to me that having another child might have helped me to get my life back on track.

Then I messed up really bad. Later in the day, I went to a store, picked up something without paying for it, got caught, and went to jail for the first time. My father was so hurt and disappointed but didn't know how he could help me.

After spending three days in jail, I was released and resumed my normal routine. Within two months, I ended up in the hospital with pneumonia. My body had endured too much trauma. I was close to death for the first time in my life, and no one thought I would recover. I was hospitalized from August 11, 1977, through September 1,1977, and was given strong antibiotics intravenously during the entire three weeks. The doctor came into my hospital room, explained how seriously ill I was, and told me I needed to stop using drugs. I wish I could tell you that I stopped using drugs and took care of my children at this point, but that is not what happened.

I recognize that God had his hands on me.

One thing that became very clear to me was that guilt and shame were present everywhere I went. These two companions of mine did not come for a visit. Instead, the pair took residence within me for years to come. The guilt from the abortions, the jail stay, and the great disappointment in my father's eyes made me feel I was doomed for disaster and that nothing and no one could stop the events that were to come upon me. I awoke each day dealing with situations as they arose, preparing for the next episode of my life.

By this time, all my classmates and friends were preparing to go to college or joining the Armed Services. My only friends were people everyone had warned me to stay away from. I didn't know why and could not understand their rejection of my friends. As an adult and a Christian, I know and understand their intentions now, but no one ever answered my question: Why?

In 1978 I got pregnant for the fourth time and decided that, by all means, I would have the child. Alfred was in a drug program and didn't believe that the baby that I was carrying was his.

It hurt me so badly that he believed I was living so wild that I would tell him it was his child when it wasn't. When Alfred said this to me, I didn't know the damage to my emotional state. I realized later that I had lost every ounce of love and respect for the man I thought I wanted to marry someday.

The drug program gave Alfred a furlough to come home. We did our thing, and I felt like I had just gotten pregnant when we finished. This man repeatedly said, "We were only together once."

This was the reason Alfred gave for not believing me. Yes, I know what you're saying; that's all it takes. Don't ask me how I knew, but I felt weird things going on in my body like there had been an explosion inside of me. I had never experienced anything like it before, and even though I had two pregnancies afterward still never felt it again. Nevertheless, Alfred kept his distance from me until the baby was born. Then finally, he admitted that my baby was his son. Too little, too late for our relationship. The gig was over.

CHAPTER 7

The Devil's Call

Before I gave birth to my son, I was alone and still needed money. I had no skills, and no one was hiring pregnant Black women in those days. My mind was moving a mile a minute, trying to figure out my next move. One afternoon, I was sitting alone when the enemy (the devil) came in and reminded me that I had old checks from an account that was now closed.

I went to the store, purchased all that I needed then gave the store the check. "Boy was that easy," I said, so I cashed three or four before the first one was returned from the bank. The store pressed charges, and I was sent a court date.

When the day arrived, I could not attend because my baby's water bag broke, and I was in the hospital. My son, Ronald, was born on January 5, 1979, but remained in the hospital for a month after birth because he was premature, weighing 4 pounds and 4 ounces. A month later, on Feb. 13, 1979, I would face a judge for my crime.

The public defender assured me that I would receive probation, and I did. The public defender neglected to tell me that the judge added six months of jail time along with the sentence stating that it appeared to him that my life was headed down the wrong path.

Wow. How could he know what I would do for the next seven years? I wish I could have gone to a program or something other than jail. I thought since this was my first serious offense, I would be eligible. Those programs were set aside for other people, though.

Immediately handcuffs were placed on my wrists, and I was hauled off to jail. Things were moving so fast that all I heard was the judge speaking as if he were looking into a crystal ball and seeing my immediate future.

I was released ninety days after my sentence. My brother's girlfriend came over with my baby an hour after I arrived home. I tried really hard to find a job while living with my sister, Shirley. However, things between my sister and her husband were getting bad, so I had to move, taking my four-month-old son to my older sister, Cynthia, who already had my daughter. There was no way for me to carry my baby up and down these streets until I found a place to live, or should I say to dwell because, as it seemed, wherever I went, I was not there very long.

The boy next door to my sister, Shirley, quickly fell in love with me. Jameson immediately paid for a room I could live in for a week until I figured out something. Jameson and I were not a couple, but he looked out for me. I knew how he felt about me, but I couldn't be to him what I believed he wanted. Things happened only because I felt obligated to him in exchange for his kindness. Where did this concept of relationship come from, I knew my thinking was off, but I know now that the enemy was adamant about destroying me and my future. One day I returned to my room to discover that someone had broken into our room and stolen all of my panties.

Needless to say, I couldn't live in that place alone. Yes, Jameson moved in, and I found myself stuck in a relationship with no feelings whatsoever for him.

Finally, I was hired at the airport, where private planes flew in to get the necessary inspection before taking another flight. My job was to do the booking for each aircraft. I would ensure that the tools and equipment used were documented for the proper plane. I also had the very important task of ensuring the mechanics' hours and minutes used to work on each plane were accurately noted. These mechanics made a lot of money per hour, and everyone would benefit at the end of the day.

One day as I came into work, the boss called me into his office. He explained that there was a lot of opportunity to make good money. After his short speech, my interpretation was that these guys were into something illegal, and if I stayed, I would end up shoved out of a plane over the ocean.

Yes, you're right. I never went back.

PART II

The Cocoon

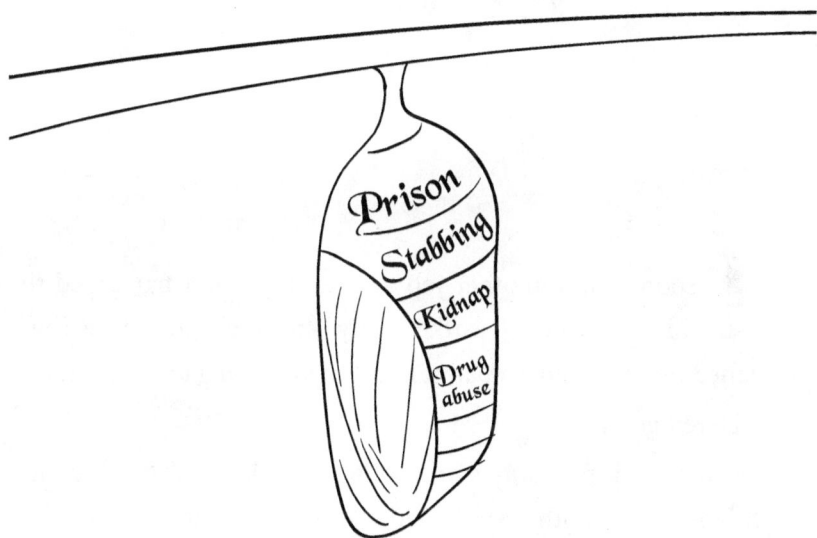

The labels on the cocoon read: Prison, Stabbing, Kidnap, Drug abuse

CHAPTER 8

My Wilderness Experience

*C*soon found another job as a waitress in a bar called the "Brew & Cue." I worked only one weekend before I was snatched up by an old acquaintance, David, ending up in Miami.

Here I go again.

David took me away from my waitress job and my situation with Jameson. Another young lady, Janine, was with me and went along for the ride. David also had a guy with him, and I could tell this other guy had his eyes on me. This was Mad Max. A guy that seemed so nice but shortly transformed into my nightmare.

We rode in a van, and Mad Max lifted a towel. Underneath were approximately twenty kilos of drugs. It was so much that I couldn't relax thinking that at any moment, someone would come with guns and kill all of us to get those drugs. I was terrified.

Fortunately, that never happened. What I can tell you is that I believe this is the place in my life where I began to pray; Lord, please help me!

When we arrived in Miami, it was mid-July of 1979. For the first few months, everyone spent a great deal of time getting to know each other. Three of us were from the same neighborhood, and this caused Mad Max to be extremely paranoid that David, Janine and I knew each other.

David and Mad Max would leave every day, saying they were out collecting money from people selling the stash (drugs) for them, but they were using all day long. Once everything was gone, David and Mad Max started cashing checks.

In the beginning, only the men would go inside the banks. But eventually, Mad Max, the one who had his eyes on me, went to jail for violating his parole, and this was when my life of check cashing began.

Boy, was I happy when Mad Max went to jail. It didn't matter where he was; I couldn't stand being around him. He was a very, very mean, nasty, evil man. The fact that he was gone was glorious. He forced me to carry knives and, at one point, made me hold one against someone's throat. The look in Mad Max's eyes let me know I had no choice. After this ordeal, prayers were a great part of my days and nights.

I knew before leaving Broward County that I was pregnant again. Mad Max thought the baby was his, and I wouldn't tell him anything different. But he was gone; I was cashing checks, working banks, and hanging paper, and money flowed well. I worked steadily, and it felt good to send money home to my sister, Cynthia, for her and the children.

In my mind, I thought that Mad Max and his meanness were out of my life forever. Even though I was getting paid illegally, I still hoped I could one day get a real job and take care of my family. These ideas seemed like a fantasy, but the hope of one day being in that good place never left me.

Early one morning, while lying in bed, my water broke again. I was only four months pregnant and immediately panicked. The other lady there, Ms. Suzy, was older, and I believed she could help me.

Instantly Ms. Suzy sprang into action, moving fast, doing things, but I can't tell you what was happening. I think I passed out. I don't remember how long, but the next thing I remember, I was shaken and asked if I was all right. I began to cry uncontrollably, saying to God that I was sorry.

As I sat crying out to God, Ms. Suzy laughed hysterically at the fact that I was asking God's forgiveness for losing my baby.

One thing I want to share is to never underestimate the emotional state of a woman who carries a child and then miscarries. Shame and guilt took control of my life once again, and I could not feel anything for a short period. No one should ever experience this.

A few days after the trauma and drama, the police arrived at the apartment to arrest Ms. Suzy. She also had warrants for check fraud. I was asked my name, and I gave them an alias because of other trouble I was in, and the cops finally left. After only twenty-four hours, Ms. Suzy was released.

One day after being out all night, I heard someone knocking on the door. I couldn't imagine who would be here so early in the morning. When I went to the door and asked who was there, I got the biggest surprise of my life.

It was Mad Max.

CHAPTER 9

Life With The Devil

Mad Max was right outside my door. He had his parole reinstated, and now my tormentor had returned, destroying every dream of escaping the crime and craziness.

Finally, I opened the door to Mad Max and looked at him, but no words would come out of my mouth.

Mad Max immediately recognized my fear and said, "Look at you. You don't know whether to hug me or to run."

Then he laughed at me. Those were my thoughts exactly. The realization that I was in full survival mode scared me, but I knew I needed to stay alert and careful with Mad Max around.

Ms. Suzy was happy he'd come back and was thinking of ways to get money for her party favors of choice. What better way for Ms.

Suzy to get close to him than to report everything I had done while he was gone for those two weeks. This could have been bad, but I didn't know enough about her to prepare for what came next.

I was asleep one morning, and Mad Max woke me up by yelling about my losing his baby. The next thing I knew, his fist hit me in the eye. I was in a terrible fog from sleeping, and I shut down completely.

Later that day, I was told to write down everything I was paid each day for cashing checks and that my numbers needed to match the guys that paid me for the money made. I will tell you right now; I threw those dudes under the bus. I never knew what pay scale was used, and I took whatever I was given. The situation came down to them or me, and I had enough.

Mad Max accepted what I said, and he and the guys decided they would all hustle more money to pay whatever was owed to me.

The next day everyone was in good spirits, and it seemed all tension was removed from the situation. The day ended extremely profitably, and all were happy. The driver of the car, who was another associate, asked to use Mad Max's car while he was having his automobile serviced.

Later in the evening, when the time came for the car to be returned, the guys were a no-show. Mad Max became very nervous, which quickly turned into venomous anger. Ms. Suzy was asked to watch for the guys and the car outside, then notify us when they returned. After about forty-five minutes, she came in to say that the car was being parked with keys in it, and both guys were leaving. Mad Max caught up with one of the guys, and they returned to the apartment.

This situation got bad very quickly. I was standing between two great big men while one held a knife and demanded all of the other's money. Yes, Mad Max robbed the other guy, and I was terrified because

I believed there was a gun in one of their pockets. I tried to speak, but no words would come out of my mouth. In a split second, I saw blood everywhere, and suddenly Mad Max wanted to get help for him.

We took the bleeding guy to the hospital and then left. While leaving, Mad Max told me that he should have killed me. I thought, "It's over for me this time," because I truly believed that no evil was beyond this man's capability and conscience. My continued silence made him angry. He had to know that I would jump at any opportunity I could to get away from him.

Once again, he read the fear in me and said, "Don't think about trying to run away from me."

Mad Max told me he would look until I was found, and things wouldn't be good for me. I knew that he would be around every corner or hiding in places he thought I may show up. I knew I didn't know many people in Opa Locka, but Mad Max knew everybody, and most people were afraid of him. It didn't matter how long it took, he would find me, so I continued praying.

For a while, things were wild and very strange. I noticed that we were followed each time Mad Max and I left the house. About three days after the robbery, Mad Max was finally apprehended by the police and would not be released this time. I was asked my name again and was told that the next time the police came there, it would be to get me.

Things were too hot there, so I took a trip back home. What started out as fun and exciting turned into the horror I thought people only read about. Yet this horror and drama were all happening to me.

CHAPTER 10

On Familiar Ground

I got on a bus and went to Cynthia's home, where my children were. I ate something, showered then had only enough strength to sleep. I never knew just how long I slept, but the next day in the afternoon, I remember waking up and seeing my sisters, Ruby and Shirley, along with my niece, Felicia, Shirley's daughter standing over me praying while my other sister, Ruby, was rubbing oil over my feet as she prayed too. I looked up at all of them, but I couldn't speak.

Then I heard Ruby say it was a good sign that I wasn't fighting. Their act of love and concern stays with me today. I am grateful that my family cared enough to come together for one purpose, with the same mind in Christ Jesus for me. I believe that I am saved today because people sacrificed. Yes, each of them put aside whatever was going on in their own lives to help a sister, living the life that chose her, who didn't know how to break free from it. These three individuals were instruments God used to bring me to Him. Thank you, Lord.

After resting for a couple of days, I began to get sick. I knew exactly what I needed. This was one of the few times I experienced withdrawals. As I got worse, I had no choice but to call my friends to pick me up so I could get what I needed. Cashing checks gave me the means to help Cynthia with my children, have a place to sleep, and maintain my acquired drug habit bigger than I.

After leaving my sister's home, I noticed something different about me. It seemed that going home had affected my life of crime. It wasn't like I could talk about it with anyone, but I needed to pay attention to what was happening. I was crying, praying, and asking God to forgive me.

After that, another great change took place. One night as I tried to sleep for hours and couldn't, I remembered that there was a Bible in the desk drawer. I removed the Bible, then placed it under my pillow. I noticed that with the Bible there, I was able to sleep. It took five years before I could sleep without the Bible under me. During the night, if the Bible would slip away, I reached and felt around until I found it and replaced it under my head. The security was real. I wasn't able yet to open the book to read, but God met me where I was spiritually.

I remained living near my sisters and children because, after all the violence I'd been through, I didn't want any chance of ever running into Mad Max again. I felt good and decided to see Alfred, my children's father. Once again, I couldn't see what was in my near future, but survival seemed to be my immediate calling.

Upon arriving, we talked for a while about the children, but most of the time, we were using drugs. I realize now that this activity was the only thing we did without fighting. I know my life sounds like one wild rodeo, but most of the things that happened to me happened quickly. I was twenty-two years old and felt like I'd lived a long, long life since my mother's passing.

At about 2 pm the next day, Alfred had a visitor. This was Friday, the day after Thanksgiving. I didn't know whether this woman, Layla, was his present girlfriend or just a friend with benefits. However, Alfred asked me not to leave and said he was only getting money from her, then Layla would be gone. Actually, I had no choice because the front door was deadbolted, and Alfred had the only key.

Alfred and his visitor, Layla, went into the backroom, where they talked for a long time while I sat patiently watching television. After a few hours, I must have fallen asleep, and Alfred woke me and asked if I'd like something to drink. I received the beverage and checked the time. I was fed up with this scene and ready to leave.

I told Alfred to unlock the door and let me out. He whispered, "Just hold on. She'll be gone soon."

I noticed that he was acting weird like maybe he had taken pills or some other drug was altering his behavior.

A moment later, Layla came out of the bedroom and said, "Do you know that everything in this apartment was purchased by me?"

I didn't respond to her because it was obvious Layla didn't know who I was to Alfred. Everyone that knew me also knew that I would fight. Trust me, if I cared for Alfred like I once had, this would have been a bad time for her. Then again, she may have felt powerful from whatever drugs they were taking. However, I felt that something bad was getting ready to take place, and I had better prepare myself. I entered the kitchen, grabbed a knife from the drawer, and placed it in my purse. One thing I knew for sure was that I was getting out of here one way or another.

About thirty minutes later, Alfred came out of the bedroom, and again I asked, "Please open the door and let me out of here, Alfred."

Again, he told me no. He would not let me leave. I lost it and started swinging the knife at him, then his girl came out, and I swung in her direction too. Suddenly, Alfred ran to the door and opened it but picked up a shovel lying in his garden by the door. He began swinging the shovel at me, forcing me back into the house. I raised my left hand to protect my face while asking him to let me go.

With my next breath ready to speak, Alfred moved out of the way, allowing me to leave. Walking down the street, I felt something warm dripping on my blouse. I stopped, looked into the glass window of a car, and saw a very big open wound in my face. I never felt the shovel touch and split my face open.

I found my way to Cynthia's house and lay down on the floor, trying my best to bleed to death. My sister returned in time, got me to the hospital and saved my life. The next morning I received a telephone call from Alfred stating that Layla had died of an apparent overdose.

As I looked at my swollen face, I only wondered why both of them weren't gone. "Stinking thinking" is the only thing that comes to mind...

CHAPTER 11

Back in the Enemy's Territory

On December 17, 1979, trouble was brewing all over Liberty City, Miami. A Black man, Arthur McDuffie, was riding his motorcycle and got into a high-speed chase with police. When the officers caught up with him, the man was beaten to death. One news report stated that Mr. McDuffie's head was cracked open like an egg.

The trial for the guilty officers began in March and was completed in April of 1980. Around May 20th of that same year, all police officers were acquitted. This sparked one of the worst racially motivated riots in Miami. The looters entered the thriving business district and set fire to almost every business on 7th Avenue. The owners of those businesses were people of color, yes, Black, law-abiding citizens that lost everything.

While many people were taking furniture, clothing, and appliances from the stores, another class of people were only interested in the checkbooks of those businesses being burned. I remember a hardware store's checks were used for almost five or six years. I probably saw what was happening on television but never realized that I was in the heart of something so awful. I couldn't feel or think about anything other than surviving another day.

I continued cashing checks and became an expert at it. I would memorize account numbers, social security numbers, and all personal information needed to provide upon request. Yes, we were making a lot of money, but as you and I both know, nothing wrong that comes fast lasts very long or is ever worth it.

On October 10, 1980, I woke up early, planning to do nothing at all, but at about 10 am, Cynthia called me for money. Normally, I would never go out cashing checks after twelve noon, but my sister with my children had a need, and I wanted to get it for her. Little did I know that I would be gone for three years when I left that day.

As I walked up to the bank, I began praying to God. "Lord, I know I am wrong and should not be here now." Immediately after I presented the check, a man came out and began chasing me. I jumped fences, cars and people and thought I had lost the man. Every time I turned around to look for this man, he was in a slow jog and was right behind me. I couldn't understand how he kept up with me at the pace he moved and how fast I ran. Later, after I had time to think, I was assured that God heard my confession. He answered me quickly.

My probation caught up with me, and I was sentenced to five years in prison. My time went very fast because I was chosen for one of the best jobs in the institution, which was water treatment. Also, since my crime wasn't violent, I was allowed to be trained in most areas of the plant, including sewer and drinking water.

Upon my release, I got reacquainted with the man who ran the check game, Calvin. In the beginning, I never did anything illegal. I had a good job working in the next county from where I lived, and Calvin continued his craft. I did not understand how important support groups were and how having a sponsor would aid in not returning to the old life I desperately wanted to be separated from.

After saving money for a while, I started to get bored. My brain was idle. I didn't really know what to make out of this new relationship with Calvin, so the enemy placed the thought of getting high in my mind. I tried to shake it off but had nothing to hold me, no one to talk with, and no one I could call to change my mind about what I was planning. Once again doing things alone and hidden out of sight.

Here I am, pretending I had my life together. It was almost like I was still the young girl maneuvering through life, praying that somehow, some way, my life would fall in line, and I would be a normal person. There was no alternate plan for me. I didn't know what was happening or where these thoughts would eventually take me.

Even though most of my sentence was finished, I was placed on parole for a short period. I decided to take a day off work, check into a motel and get high all day, thinking no one would ever know. Calvin noticed a lump sum of money was missing from the bank. I confessed that I took and used it.

Calvin asked me to please not sneak around, and if I was going to use it again, do it at home. Now that I was using it, I felt obligated to cash checks to cover the money I spent.

A very important reason I so easily returned to my misery was that I was not renewing my mind with positive information, and I didn't know God's promises. I didn't surround myself with any type of support system and thought by some miracle that those behaviors and mindsets would all just disappear.

Unfortunately, this was not the plan God had set in place. The answers to the things destroying us won't be found in those being ruined. We must seek counsel outside ourselves with those who have successfully transitioned from darkness to the light of life. That light being Jesus Christ, the light of the world.

One morning Calvin and I rose early because we had planned a busy day. I don't remember why, but we began to argue about something. This was normally a bad sign because we were not in harmony. However, we went to the bank anyway, I was arrested, and this cycle continued.

In jail again, my mind was racing because my friend only had a few hours to get me bonded out before the system picked my name as being on parole. Finally, I was released, but I was afraid to return to my job, thinking that I would be arrested there when my P.O. (parole officer) found out what I was doing. I started running. Calls came to my house and Cynthia's house, pleading with me to just call my officer.

I never did. This was a very bad mistake.

'Opa-locka 200' check-forgers bilking millions from banks, public, police say

By NANCY LAUGHLIN
Herald Staff Writer

A sophisticated gang of more than 200 check-forgers, runners and dealers in stolen checks has bilked banks and the public from the Treasure Coast to Dade County out of millions of dollars during the past decade.

Police in a dozen South Florida counties are keeping their eye on the gang, known as "the Opa-locka 200" because its roots are in the Northwest Dade suburb.

Hounded in Dade and Broward counties by detectives who keep scrapbooks on the members, the Opa-locka 200 now are focusing their attention on Martin and Palm Beach counties. "That is relatively virgin territory up there," said Pompano Beach police detective Darryl Marshall.

"I would estimate in the last three or four years, they've taken probably $1.5 million around here," Marshall said. "Combined in Dade and Broward counties, it's probably $3 million over the last six or seven years."

Although the gang's membership constantly changes, police say, it is a highly sophisticated organization. It provides training for new members, experts who manufacture phony IDs, and a clearinghouse in Opa-locka through which members and other gangs buy, sell and exchange stolen blank checks.

The gang's favorite ploy involves a scam known as "split-depositing," police said. Gang members obtain information about the checking accounts of ordinary people, steal their signatures and then use them to cash blank checks stolen from businesses.

Typically, a gang member will pose as a bank customer, take the check to a branch of the bank other than the one ordinarily visited by the customer, deposit a small part of the check and walk out with the remainder in cash.

The bank is stuck with the bad check. The real bank customer is not liable for the stolen cash.

Stuart detective Sgt. Joan Waldron said there are many ways that gang members can obtain the information necessary to their scam.

"They'll steal bill payments out of the mail," take down the account number, photocopy the signature nd then mail the payment on its v. Condominiums that have unlocked boxes into which ts can toss outgoing mail are 'gets, she said.

'so go behind banks at through dumpsters," 'gt: Ralph Nelson of County Police De onomic Crimes Unit. banks shred their

'They're eating us alive.'

Liz Cline, sheriff's detective

Cancer Society spokesman said.

Also passed were checks stolen, four years ago from the now-defunct DTC Realty Co., once located at the corner of 27th and 54th streets in the heart of the 1980 riots.

'Checks all over the place'.

"I can't tell you how many times I've been subpoenaed for bad checks," said Andrew DeWitt, an official of the DTC Tool Co., a sister company of the out-of-business real estate firm. "We were burned out. Since then, our checks are all over the place. There are literally hundreds of them."

DeWitt said looters also stole payroll checks and records, which enabled forgers to make identification cards used in cashing the checks.

Police said the stolen checks often pass through a clearinghouse in Opa-locka. "Dade County and federal agents know where the house is, but they've never been able to shut it down," because they lack sufficient evidence to raid it, Pompano's Marshall said.

Investigators believe the house is "used for storing the checks until they're not hot any more," Marshall said.

Martin County sheriff's detective Charles Jones added: "If you have the right connections, you can come from anywhere and buy checks from them."

On the Treasure Coast, police said members walked into the Zayre department store on U.S. 1 in Stuart and simply helped themselves to a handful of check-cashing verification cards the store keeps in cardboard boxes on an office count-

er.

All the cards taken were for customers with last names that began with the letter "A." Within days, checks from DTC Realty, the American Cancer Society and other Miami companies began moving through those customers' Treasure Coast bank accounts.

Among them were the Florida National Bank and Trust Co. accounts of Kay Kellogg Ash and Gale Allison, both of Martin County.

One of the bad-check counts Gillens faces involves a Cancer Society check made out to Ash. Gillens allegedly filled in the amount for $564.80, then forged Ash's endorsement. Court affidavits state she then deposited the check and got back $400 in cash.

"They're very smart," said Ash, a 34-year-old marketing representative. "I live in Palm City, and it's the only Florida National branch in the county they didn't pass a check at. In the course of eight days, this person had taken about $3,200 through my account."

Allison, a former teacher, said the was astounded at the forgers' expertise. "The forgery on my checks was very good. I almost could have sworn I'd signed it myself."

Although the banks, not the account holders, bear the loss, "it's such a violation. It's like you've been raped or something," Ash said. "The fact that somebody else knows how to sign your name, knows your address and phone number — it makes you want to keep all the curtains closed."

Membership changing

Despite continual arrests, police said they have little hope of stopping the group — or several bands of other forgers in the state — for good. Nelson, who began keeping a scrapbook of gang members' pictures and forgery work in 1974, said he has more than 150 photographs. But the gang's membership is constantly changing, he said.

And those who have been sent to

prison "get to one to three years most of the time," Marshall said. "They're usually out on the streets in a year or so."

Palm Beach County's Cline said a major problem in prosecution is that police have had no network to prove that a chain of forgeries in several locations has occurred, so "every check comes up on its own merit."

Police in several locations are waging their war against forgers with economic crimes units, which cooperate with one another and with businesses to keep records and exchange information about the forgers. Three now operate in the state — in Dade County, Palm Beach County and on the Treasure Coast.

Information from the crime units is credited with helping police make the Treasure Coast arrests. Police said they are determined to continue circulating information about the Opa-locka 200 until every department in the state knows about the gang and its methods.

During an economic crimes seminar for police and businesses in Palm Beach last week that attracted more than 300 participants, "the gang's name came up more than once," Marshall said. Said the Fort Lauderdale investigator: "We're going to keep after them."

Indeed, Cline said, police will have no choice. "Now that things are hot in Dade and Fort Lauderdale," she said with a sigh, "we're getting a heavy concentration of them in Pompano Beach, Delray Beach, Martin County and as far west as St. Petersburg. They are saturating the whole state."

Herald Staff Writer Jean Chance contributed to this report.

CHAPTER 12

Trying To Break Free

So, after my time in prison for fraud and my release in May 1983. I worked at that good and legitimate job for approximately six months before my old habits resurfaced. Those same habits gave me the same results, prison.

In April of 1984, the team of check cashers were arrested in north Florida. Calvin and I were on the team. Detectives were at another bank across the street from a bank I came out of investigating the checks cashed weeks before. Officers noticed our car with a Broward County tag as I was coming out of the bank. No one inside the bank knew the checks I had just cashed were fraudulent. The detective began questioning me about what I might have been doing. This is where the final chapter of my life of crime would soon end, but I wasn't quite done yet.

After being in jail for a week or two, I asked for a newspaper and was told that inmates were not allowed to read the news. Soon all charges were dropped on my partner, Calvin, but he was transferred to another jail where more check charges were waiting for him. As soon as Calvin arrived there, he wrote me a letter explaining that our names had been in the papers for about a week, referring to us as part of "The Opa Locka 200" check cashing ring.

The 200 was an estimate of the number of members involved. I called my dad, and he was angry with me. He told me that I should have gotten married and changed my name so as not to be associated with him. I believe that my father was sorely embarrassed. And guess what? I was pregnant again.

These ladies came to the jail cell for Bible study. Everyone would sit together at the table. I never chose to attend. However, this one lady, Ms. Nancy, would always—I mean always—come over to speak to me. I assumed she was some over-zealous Christian, you know, overdoing her part. Her questions had a definite agenda, I now know.

Eventually, she began writing to me, and we became pen pals. I started sitting in the Bible study groups, and Ms. Nancy was always very concerned and focused on my baby and me. It wasn't long before she told me that she knew of a good family if I ever needed someone to care for my child. I was only there in her city jail for four months, but it was long enough for her to plant the seeds she desired.

Ms. Nancy reminded me in every letter that she had someone to take my baby. I saw her words but never thought about it. I had other pressing things going on, like court appearances, adjusting to being back in jail, and, more importantly, wondering how long I would be away from my children this time. The thought of having another child began to consume every waking moment.

I received a four-year sentence, of which I would serve only two years because the crime I committed was, again, a non-violent one, so I was eligible for all good behavior time offered.

CHAPTER 13

Exodus: From Darkness to Light

I gave birth to my son, Calvin, at the outside hospital, meaning I was taken from prison to an outside hospital. Calvin, the baby's father, did come for a visit and to sign his birth certificate. He gave me no information about his mother or her promise to care for our son. I needed to make decisions fast before my child was hauled off to foster care. I never asked my family because Cynthia already cared for two of my children. I just could not bring myself to put more responsibility upon her with another child.

I thought maybe the family Ms. Nancy spoke to me about was available. I called her, and the couple was there to take my child away within the hour. I cried out loud, saying I wasn't leaving until the next day, and they agreed to return. Early the following morning, the couple was there and gone with my baby so fast that I could not even process what had taken place until I was back at the prison. This all happened on December 1, 1984.

I was released in the summer of 1986. On my first day home, I asked a relative to take me to the other side of town in hopes of checking on a few jobs when I was driven to a dope hole (a place where people get high on drugs). I didn't want to be there, but there was no restraint or power not to use it again. While incarcerated, I had to attend Narcotics Anonymous by force, not by choice. I wondered how my relatives knew I had plenty of money in my purse. Addicts can sense these things.

Now there I was again, falling prey to the weakness preventing me from returning with my children. How could I go get my baby boy, Calvin, back? I called the couple and explained my drama and, to my surprise, was told that they didn't want me to get him. I assured them I would come for my son as soon as I got straight. I never knew anything about these people, only that they would help me. The couple told me the door would always be open, and I believed them.

The couple reached out to my other children. My daughter, Antoinette and oldest son, Ronald, were picked up and taken to visit Calvin in their home. Antoinette was about seven years old at the time. After observing her surroundings, she called Cynthia and told her that she was not being fed, that they had not taken a bath, and

Exodus: From Darkness to Light

that she was ready to come home. After Antoinette got off the telephone, the couple told her that she was not being mistreated but that they just lived differently. Also, my little girl was told that her entire conversation with my sister was recorded, which sealed Antoinette's desire to get out of there and back home.

This was when my mind and spirit began to grieve. I started seeing and feeling the hurt and pain of how my decisions and behavior affected my family. I couldn't imagine what little Calvin was experiencing because I knew nothing about this family other than that they obviously loved and cared for my son. Needless to say, Ronald and Antoinette never visited my youngest son again.

Every conversation when I called home, Antoinette constantly said to me, "Momma, please go and get Calvin. I don't like the way he's being treated." These words echoed in my ears and heart for a long time. What could I do? How could I do anything with this new habit?

One day in April of 1987, the hunger to be with my children and family became overwhelming. I remember having quiet moments and crying to the Lord, asking Him to help me. I told Him I didn't believe I was born to have a life like this. My heart was extremely heavy from that day on, but I did experience a peace within that let me know that the way I was living would soon come to an end. My conscience and spirit were troubled like never before. Each moment of every day, I was tormented by thoughts of what a mess I'd made of my life. I felt at one point that my situation was impossible to correct. Guilt and shame reminded me of some things I did in the presence of people that would always remember those acts.

At this stage, I couldn't be too concerned about tomorrow because today, I had to deal with the chemical need that my body must have for me to function, drugs.

In October 1987, I was arrested once again for a misdemeanor. However, it took three days to get my first court appearance. I couldn't imagine why it took so long to get there. But this time, I felt relieved about being in jail. Something was very different. Normally I would call my friends to get me out, but I had quiet patience as never before. I was very familiar with the routine in the jail as it relates to court procedures. I soon discovered that two banks were collaborating and filing charges against me. When I saw the information, I learned the dates and the information were filed on me back in April. Yes, that was when I prayed to God, asking for deliverance and salvation.

Immediately He answered. God does answer sinners' prayers!

The trial began about five months after I was arrested. The prosecutor offered a plea bargain of seven years. It sounded good, but a voice inside me said, "Taking a plea bargain? Are you trying to control your own affairs? Release. Let go and let God have His way." So I meditated on it for a while, and though it was hard, I decided to try God.

The jury returned with a guilty verdict, and I was sentenced to seventeen years. I thought I had made a terrible mistake, but this was not the case. The decision turned out to be one of the best decisions I've ever made.

After carefully calculating the approximate amount of time I would serve, I prayed and said to the Lord, "God, if this is the time that you need to work a miracle for me, I give you every day. Please show me how to live according to your will and your way."

I ended up only serving four years of the seventeen-year sentence. My restoration of life began, and it has been amazing!

I would call my father each Sunday morning, excited about what I heard in church and how God was changing my life. He was so happy for me and told me he truly hoped I had learned my lesson.

One Sunday morning, August 13, 1989, I called home to speak with my father as I did every week and learned that while I was on the phone, my father lay in his bed, cold. He passed away that morning, and I grieved at his passing because I knew he would never see the Lord's answer to his prayers concerning me.

Not having my father any longer caused me to really take a good look at myself. I journeyed back through my past, acknowledged where I was—in prison—and began to develop a vision for my future right there. Sadness came over me like a terrible storm, crying for hours, not knowing how to begin straightening the terrible mess I'd made for myself and my three children.

My relationship with the Savior was my comfort and security. Each time my cellmate left, I would take the opportunity to get on my knees to pray. I also woke early in the mornings, at about five o'clock each day, to invite God into my life and decision-making. At this point, I knew no one else could help fix my situation. I truly believed with all my heart that Christ came into me to live and guide me through this world.

The Lord began answering prayers, and I recognized my faith in Him increasing. I needed to try Jesus, this time giving Him all of me and my complete attention. Soon others who were also incarcerated began to notice my relationship. Often, they would come to me to talk about what was going on back at their homes with their children and sometimes what transpired within our prison walls.

I knew that God's Word brought comfort in any and all situations. I did my absolute best to encourage and remind them that we must put our hope and trust in the Lord for the next phase of our lives. We all agreed that doing what put us in chains could not be the blueprint for our future. After speaking with someone about salvation, I would sit amazed at the words that came out of my mouth. God was truly changing me!

While serving my last sentence, God privileged me by getting into a paying job assignment. I made forty-five cents an hour, which paid me twenty-five dollars every two weeks. It was just what I needed. Yes, I needed to be able to handle this time independently, not call home asking for help. Don't misunderstand me; my family didn't have an issue helping me, but I wanted to continue learning how to be a mature, responsible adult in God's way. So I also got jobs on the side ironing clothes for those who could afford to pay.

Upon my release, the work program aided me in finding employment in the field of work that I did while incarcerated. I worked for that company for eight years before finding a better-paying job doing the same work. I would work at this new place for eleven years. This company was bought out and sold, and I experienced unemployment for about six months before I was rehired by another company. All I can say is that God restored everything I thought was lost forever during those years.

The Lord was dealing with me concerning what I studied in His Word. I asked Him to give me the power to obey all I understood to be a command. I never knew what power resided inside me until I encountered the Spirit of God concerning fornication.

PART III

The Butterfly

CHAPTER 14

Transformation

pproximately one month after coming home for good, Calvin asked me to marry him. I said yes but felt very strange after I responded. I couldn't explain what was happening to me. All I knew was that I had no choice but to trust God for what I needed Him to do in my life. When Calvin gave me the engagement ring, I accepted but insisted we wait another year before we started counseling.

Being convicted to live holy unto God with my body was a command I wasn't sure I could obey. After all, having sex had been a part of my life for so long that living abstinent did not compute.

Calvin and I went to a motel to attempt sex, but we both knew our time together was not the same. He shrugged it off as nerves and jitters, but I knew exactly who it was. God!

Three weeks later, after planning a night out to the movies and dinner, we ended up at another motel. I didn't feel comfortable doing this, but I wasn't aware of the power within me to say no. My flesh was fighting me, and my mind reminded me that I'd been with this man for eight years, so what could be wrong?

Upon arriving there, I laid down across the bed, relaxing. My fiancé left the room to use the telephone. I started thinking, "Why did I agree to this?" I knew that I should not have been there.

At that moment, in the twinkling of an eye, I saw a soldier. Standing at least eight feet tall, he was fully armored, helmet, breastplate, etc. His right arm, with his fist closed, was across his chest. I jumped up from the bed, got into the shower, and as the water ran over me, I heard a voice speaking to me, saying, "You will no longer know this man as you have before and will not have both my Son and fiancé at the same time."

I don't remember any other things said, but I immediately dressed and demanded I be taken home.

All this happened on December 7, 1991. Calvin and I continued the relationship without fornication. It was hard at first because he just thought I had someone else, but he soon realized that it was God changing me. Later he told me that he saw me changing every day before his eyes and wondered how he could stop doing some of the things he was involved in.

My response to him was that I gave up trying to fix my life and decided to try the LORD.

On December 31, 1991, I was invited to what the church called a "Watch Night" service held at Koinonia Worship Center, where Calvin attended. This was not my first invitation, but I decided to accept and not avoid it any longer.

My hesitation in attending was all about my past, my actions, and the folks that witnessed my madness. I never wanted to interact with people in my community again. How did Calvin end up in a church in my old neighborhood? The thought of facing my peers and their parents was scary for me, but this was home.

I knew and believed God forgave me, but fear took precedence over knowledge. Even though I agreed to attend, I came in, and the first seat I saw was in the last row in the back of the church. This was perfect.

The service was very inspiring, and the message was encouraging for all I was experiencing then. It was almost as if the speaker knew something about me and had known I would be there.

One part of the service recognized the members who passed on to heaven. I was touched deeply by the reverence and respect given to those individuals. Sitting there in the back row, I felt something happening inside me. I was being filled, and the presence of God was near to me. A change was taking place, and the best way to describe this is like having huge arms hugging and comforting me while at the same time assuring me that I would be all right.

At the end of the service, as the invitation for salvation or membership was offered, I got out of my seat and found myself standing in front of the entire church. This was a huge congregation; honestly, I don't remember the long walk from the last row. However, something was special about this place, and I needed to be there.

After returning to my seat, I sat quietly, trying to internalize what was happening inside me. Calvin apparently sensed something also, but he never interfered with my moment.

After the service ended, we were invited to breakfast at the home of one of the members. Sister Addie Mitchell loved to cook and entertain God's people. The fellowship was so sweet, and I felt honored to be with my brother and sister. Once there, I realized that Sister Mitchell was my classmate's mother. She became a mentor and friend at that breakfast, and we are still close today.

Calvin and I never spoke or had any conversation about our son. He was still angry with me for allowing the family to take him without discussing the matter with him. Each time I attempted to bring our son up in conversation, I felt something on the inside telling me, "Not now."

I was living in Fort Lauderdale, Florida, where I secured employment at Advantage Optical. I worked there for eight years.

I also started attending Bible study on Thursday nights. I needed the van to pick me up because I had no car. This worked for a while but using the church van to drive that far, approximately 20-25 miles for one person, was not a good idea.

God sent me two angels who saw me and decided to make the sacrifice of driving the long distance to pick me up, and if we didn't find anyone going in my direction, those two would drive me all the way home. Today because of their sacrifice, I have grown into a person like them. Through the years, I have always made myself available to bring people to church in the hope of those individuals finding the treasure I found in Jesus Christ. Sacrificing like the couple that took a leap of faith for me. Thank you, Mr. and Mrs. Sparks.

For the next year and a half, I studied God's Word, joined the Women God Can Use Ministry, and became a facilitator. God was truly using me, and I continued to surrender to Him.

Calvin and I remained friends, attending church and movies and restaurants. But for one reason or another, our lives were growing further apart. At one point, I felt that I wanted to stop trying to keep up. However, something inside me told me I must continue, and I needed to trust God.

I remember being baptized when I was maybe nine or ten, but a strong desire gripped me tightly, and I believed that understanding the process should come first. So on May 2, 1993, I was baptized again, completing my salvation process. Amen.

On August 11, 1993, I received a telephone call that my son's father, Calvin, had died from an apparent drug overdose. I was shocked to learn that he was found in the same motel we were in on December 7, 1991, when I saw the vision and heard a voice speak to me.

Lord, I'm so grateful that I chose to obey you. I was deeply hurt, and although I believed God was perfect in all His ways, I still couldn't understand why my friend had to die. Nevertheless, I concluded that I would understand things better in time.

When we ask the Lord to do things in our life, we must let go. God's way is perfect, and as we continue to live, He begins to show us, little by little, why. My dreams of sitting around the table one day telling our children how the Lord delivered us together were gone. I know now that my ways were not God's ways at all. Amen!

In 1995 my Aunt Ruby, my dad's sister, was diagnosed with Alzheimer's and needed to be cared for. Yes, my sister was named after our aunt. With everything I was dealing with concerning my children, I didn't see how I could take on any more responsibility. I brought my aunt to live with me, but she wanted to be in her own house. I felt the Lord directing me to do whatever was needed for my aunt.

Preparing the home for my family to make an exodus was difficult. It took over a year to renovate the living areas and lots of money. God provided the entire supply of what was needed. Once Aunt Ruby knew I would be there with her, she felt better. Soon I fell right back into my role of serving. Surprisingly, throughout my nine years of serving my aunt, I began to think restoration was possible. During those years of serving, I was extremely blessed and felt privileged to be able to help in such a meaningful way.

I must tell everyone that the Lord sent an angel to me to help care for Aunt Ruby. Her name is Sister Maxine Phelps. God used Mrs. Phelps to help me as well. The responsibility was great, and she, alongside me, eliminated stressful situations. Thanks again.

God called Aunt Ruby home in 2003, and I wouldn't have dreamed I would miss her as I have. I understand some things better each day as I walk with the Lord.

CHAPTER 15

Taking Back What is Mine by God's Grace

One day I felt empowered and had a great sense of freedom. Now was the time for all my children to be brought home. I called and spoke with the couple, telling them I wanted my son. I didn't know the greatest fight of my life would begin. My fight was spiritual; I had to say what I needed and then wait on God. This was extremely hard for me because, at any time, I could have just gone to their home and taken my son. But the Lord told me He would do this for me. My job was to wait and stay in my lane, praying, trusting, and believing that if God said it, it was already done.

The family told me I couldn't get my son because they did not know how I lived. I never gave them custody, but I needed to be careful not to get in God's way. He didn't need my help to accomplish His Word. My correspondence with the family continued for about eight months.

A visit was planned, and this was special on so many levels. My son was now nine years old, and it had been about five years since I'd seen him. The first visit took place in October of 1994. At that time, the foster dad told me his family wanted to adopt my child. He also told me he wanted to take my son out of the country. The foster dad couldn't take my son with him if he didn't have custody. I reminded them that my intentions were never to give my son away. The foster dad expressed how much he loved my son and desired to raise him as his own child. He held my son's arms out to let me see his little muscles, describing how well he had cared for Calvin. This bothered me because of how my son was held, and the gesture made me remember how slaves were sold. This image has never left me. I'm sorry if I seem to be overreacting but remember, this is my truth.

I reminded the foster dad that I was told I could get my son anytime I wanted, and now was that time. I refused any more discussion about adoption. Therefore, this ended our visit.

I returned home, and after a few weeks, I wrote another letter explaining that I wanted to bring my son home to meet his family. Three weeks passed, and I hadn't heard anything from the foster family. This was strange because our correspondence was always good. Then one day, the letter I wrote to the family was returned to me with their forwarding address. This made me feel that the family was attempting to disappear with my son. But God! Someone in the postal service placed their forwarding address on my letter and returned it to me. So I changed the envelope and resent my letter. Yes, I feel that the family was planning something because the foster mom called me very angry, asking, "How did you get that address? Those people don't want you writing there." As I listened to her, I couldn't understand her anger, then without me having a chance to respond, she said that the foster dad was scheduling another visit.

The visit was scheduled for Saturday, February 25, 1995. The day before the visit, at about 4 pm in the afternoon, I received a call from the foster dad stating, "While he was praying, God told him to give me my child." The next day when I made the two-hour drive to get my son, I was told that after the school year ends, the child would decide with whom he wanted to live. The decision was made when the Lord told the family to give me my child. And there's this law that children do not make these decisions. I knew once I got my child home, I had no intention of him returning to live as their son in their home ever again.

Nevertheless, as I gathered my son's things before leaving, the foster dad gave me a legal document with the name Isaiah Bell. The birthday was correct, but the birth year made my child a year younger than he actually was. I didn't understand what all this was for, but I needed to put this aside for the moment. I enrolled my son in school with his birth name and correct date of birth. This document stated that my child was exempt from all vaccinations. So the fact that my son has never been called by the name I gave him at birth bothered me because now, after being known as Isaiah all nine years, he has to be called Calvin. God has promised not to leave me or forsake me. I believe you, Lord! Mentally and emotionally, this is bad for my child, and I'm so hurt by what's happening to him. God will not leave my son or me to go through this alone!

Heavenly Father, forgive me for what I have done. My sin is always before me, and I confess that I have been wrong. Thanks for your forgiveness.

CHAPTER 16

Standing in the Fire

Our home life was bombarded by telephone calls and unannounced visits by this group of White folks that tried to make me feel guilty about taking Calvin from the family. These White men were at least fifty-five to sixty years of age. Many women called my home, but only the men came to my house. I cried before the Lord feeling that I was being disrespected because I was a single, Black woman and didn't have a man to stand up for me. God assured me that He was the man to deal with this situation, so I endured the necessary drama.

Calvin's school year ended quickly, as did our summer. I was excited as all the children were for the new school year. We purchased new shoes, clothes, book bags, and pencils, everything we thought would be needed for the upcoming school term. I was receiving money from Social Security from my son's father's benefits.

Concerning the foster family, I instructed Calvin to inform me each time he was contacted by his other family whenever I wasn't home. Apparently, they advised him to do the opposite, and my son obeyed them.

As the sun rose, so did I. I was just as excited as the children were, having everyone together where we could be a family. I entered Calvin's bedroom to wake him, and he was gone!

Immediately, I called the police and was told someone would contact me soon. When I got to work, a detective from the Missing Persons Unit called and asked me several questions. I explained my situation to her and gave her every telephone number I found among Calvin's things. The forged and illegal document from his other family was among the information provided. As retaliation for sharing this with the police, I was reported to the Social Security Administration for receiving payments while not yet having custody of my son.

This was an attempt to disqualify me as a good parent and possibly place me in prison again. Maybe the family felt they could regain custody of Calvin without issue if this happened to me.

The detective called me back within an hour to say they had my son. Calvin was told to leave my home, call the foster parents and wait until his foster dad drove two hours to pick him up. The detective also called the local police to find out who these people were.

This is when I found out that this family was Amish. Initially, the detective wanted to drive up to get Calvin, but the family insisted on bringing him home. The time was set, and the detective came to my home to monitor the drop-off. When they didn't show up after an hour, the detective decided to leave. She asked me to call her if they showed up. Not quite ten minutes after she left, my local police department called to say that I could come there to pick Calvin up. Immediately I called the detective, she returned, picked me up and went off to the station. Once there, she told me to take Calvin home and never let him go back.

After that incident, the family slowed things down but kept the pressure on trying to convince me that adoption was best. I could not understand why the family didn't believe I could care for Calvin now. Was it that it took nine years for my transformation to take place? I didn't know. Their faith and testimony were similar to mine, but for some reason, they didn't believe that the God who delivered them had not done the same for me.

The foster dad and I went to counseling with my pastor, and at the end of every session, I said, "No, you can't adopt my son. I never told you that was an option."

The family's pursuit was extremely intense. On some Sundays, I would be in worship service, and this man would come to where Calvin and I were sitting and start hugging and kissing my son. I thought he was trying to convince my entire church that my son would be better off with him. God only knew my torment. My past failures as a mother were being paraded over the entire church and community. I couldn't be concerned about what "people" thought and said about me. The important thing was to keep my eyes on my situation and watch my God fix it! Amen.

There is so much going on in my life at this time. I believe every prayer warrior was calling my family's name in their prayers. I was being tried by the fires I started and knew that deliverance would one day be ours. I'm still trusting in the one that made the promise to give me back my family.

Calvin went a while without seeing his foster family. I never wanted to alienate Calvin from them, but their disrespect for me made it impossible to deal with them on their terms. I agreed that the family would visit with Calvin in a public place in the exact way that I was permitted to visit.

In March of the following year, Calvin asked me if he could go for a visit while on spring break. I didn't mind because, as I said before, I never intended to sever ties with them; I just needed time and space for Calvin to see how the rest of the world was living. After the involvement with the police, I hadn't been bothered much, only by telephone.

At the end of Calvin's visit, he called me and said his foster dad was not bringing him back home. Now by this time, my son really liked being here with his brother, sister, and cousins. Also, I was reminded that these people tape all conversations, and since Calvin knew this, he chose his words carefully and quickly so I would understand that he did not want to stay there.

I assured Calvin that I was on my way. The foster dad took the telephone away from Calvin and told me I should not try to come there because they were in the woods and I could get lost. I told him I believed I would have no problem locating them.

As I was preparing to leave, something inside me said to go to the church to let someone know where I was going. I spoke to one of my pastor's wives, and after I explained what was happening, she decided to go with me. She went inside to tell her husband, and he agreed to come along. My friendship with this family continues today. I'm so grateful to the Pastor and Sister Diane Smith for their availability and willingness to help me through this time. These individuals walked what they talked. Whatever the need was, they would sacrifice to help anyone.

When we arrived, I saw Calvin coming out of what looked like some sort of stable on a ranch. The pastor got out of the car to let everyone know I was not alone. That seemed to disrupt their intentions. A White male I had never met told the pastor my son would be right out. When my child finally reached my car, he was very sad. His eyes were puffy from crying. Calvin said nothing, only laid down and went to sleep, relieved to finally be free.

I couldn't get over the feeling I had in my spirit as I was backing out to leave. Something came over me that made me feel that if I had gone alone, no one would have ever seen me again. I believed that I had just escaped death. After that, Calvin never went for another visit until he was ready to graduate from high school.

After all that our family went through with the foster family, getting settled took a lot of prayer and focus. We all continued our daily routines, and l felt we were growing as a family.

However, I recognized that my older son, Ronald, raised by my sister, Cynthia, was beginning to act out. I knew that this situation with Calvin had distracted me from other things I should have been watching with Ronald.

This reminded me again that God's way was right, and my way was wrong. I mean that it takes a mother and a father to raise children. Being a single, unmarried parent creates an unstable environment that produces many problems. Children often grow up lacking important qualities that the family structure would have produced.

As soon as I recognized where Ronald was mentally and emotionally, I sought help from every place possible. Everyone came and spent time encouraging Ronald and doing different things to aid in correcting the path my oldest son was on.

Alfred, Ronald's father, had excuse after excuse after excuse for why he would not help me with his child. He gave money, but his time was what was needed.

After exhausting every possible option I had, I prayed. God was waiting with open arms for me. Just when I was about to lose hope, the Lord stepped into our situation.

After Ronald landed in prison at seventeen years old and returned to me at twenty-two, I was just grateful we survived. Now at forty-two, he is the man I knew he wanted to be.

Calvin, my youngest son, went through the Right of Passage at my church, where young men are mentored and guided into manhood. After graduation, he went to college on a wrestling scholarship. After two years, he returned home and then went back to his foster family.

Recently, Calvin called me to say, "Mom, I'm so glad you fought for me."

I reminded Calvin that I always loved him and that giving him away was never my intention. Calvin's gratitude does not release me from the sadness of knowing what he experienced at such a young age wasn't all good. However, the God that we serve will make it work together for our good because we love Him. I will continue to pray that Calvin will one day soon experience true freedom found in Jesus Christ, seeking God's deliverance from any bondage he finds himself in today due to what he went through.

At thirty-eight years old, I believe Calvin is now recognizing what I and others have been ministering to him all along. The message has been that the Lord wants glory and honor from the testimonies that we have been given. I know that when Calvin receives his freedom, he will tell his complete testimony of his life from birth to nine and the drama of adjusting to us, his biological family. I'm sure my son longed to return to what he was used to at the beginning of his life and hated me for disrupting his family. However different our lives were, God gave Calvin to me, and I loved my son and never intended to give my child away. My life and the life we lived differently wasn't what he wanted. I would like to hear what Calvin says, but his words will never be for my hearing. I'm all right with what God alone is doing in the hearts of His children. Thank you, Lord, for your long-suffering and patience with me as I am now completing the work set before me. I thank you for seeing something in me worth saving.

I have questions about this entire situation.

Why did the foster family want to take my son out of the country? Why did the foster family change Calvin's birth name? Why was the birth year changed on the legal document? Thinking of all that has taken place, I'm troubled.

My truth: I believe that if my son had been taken out of the country with the incorrect name and date of birth, he would have turned up missing. My heart is saddened by this truth. I believe this situation is bigger than I could have ever imagined.

Hundreds of pregnant women each year come into prisons with no one to care for their children. How many of their children have been taken out of the country and never heard from again.

I wonder if anyone has ever researched what happened to all of the children of women in prisons. If an incarcerated woman makes an agreement solely between the mother and a foster family with no agency monitoring the children after the papers are signed, who is watching to make sure these children are not trafficked? I know for a fact many of these women could have life sentences or very long sentences. Something deep inside of me causes me to feel sick thinking how easily predators could have a successful business selling children from incarcerated mothers.

The document with my son's fictitious name stated that he was exempt from any shots or vaccinations to attend school. To me, this means no DNA. As I put the facts together

1. Fictitious Name

2. Fictitious Birth year

3. Fictitious Parent Name

4. No DNA

5. Wants to take a child out of the country

I believe that this could very well be a formula for any child to disappear. If my child had been missing, there is no way I would have found him. This is what I believe God saved my child from. Yes, God saved Calvin from being another missing child.

My son and his godfather

Pamela (me) with Calvin

CHAPTER 17

Goodbye Shame

We all were born in sin, alienated away from the presence of the Almighty Jehovah. The crucified Savior, the blood that was shed, allows your good works to be seen. But good deeds alone can't save anyone.

Remember, God promised us eternal life with Him. I believe wholeheartedly that I will live forever in His peaceful presence. I am fully persuaded that every iota of His divine word is true. His Spirit lives inside me and testifies to this truth continuously: that God shall perform every promise concerning those belonging to Him. Amen.

Humbly I served my brothers and sister with love to demonstrate that I was no longer who I used to be. This ungodly thinking placed me in another arena of bondage. The reality is that

I gained nothing but wasted a lot of precious time fulfilling other folks' needs. My humility became an exposed weakness. Please recognize that the Lord wants to benefit from your life. In the beginning, I felt God was with me while I served. However, I know today that He never intended me to be in that space for as long as I stayed.

Another aspect of my humility was self-condemnation. My thoughts of my past self would not allow me to tap into the greatness of my purpose. Because these thoughts were private, I felt no need to share what was happening inside me.

I never blamed other people, but it was in a different way, confirming the lie my mind was telling me. Saying, I don't belong, you can do this or that but remember what you have done, and we haven't forgotten. Now I don't believe that things were said verbally, but the enemy had enough going on to keep me in check, so to speak.

The shame of what other people have seen me do has held me captive. I would communicate and seek fellowship, but then at some point, I would regress and vanish from sight. Sometimes I felt that others' behaviors triggered negative thoughts instead of a resounding atmosphere of love and the peace that the ground at the foot of the cross is level. I needed every person who touched me or my situation to believe and trust me. My displaced feelings were because of what was going on inside me. I knew my view of things was distorted, and things weren't as they seemed. So I charged everything to my overreacting, giving everyone else the benefit of the doubt concerning whatever matter was before me. This always helped me to maintain my altitude.

The response from the Lord to what was going on in my thoughts was found in 1 Peter 2:9. Every child of God is unique and a part of His royal priesthood. My understanding of what God's word was telling me is that I, and those like me, saved and delivered from sin, would never fit into any environment that is in and the birth of this world. Our DNA is holy, righteous, and heaven-bound. We are literally passing through, and our roots are planted in Jesus Christ, who alone has our home prepared so we can be with Him forever!

So, my dear sisters and brothers, when you feel overlooked and excluded from the hoopla in the church, work, school, etc., please understand that our God doesn't want us to blend in with the crowds. I believe He desires us to be different and stand up for holiness. It's an honor to be separated from anything that refuses to give Him all glory.

Just think about it. When God blesses His children, we are never excluded from the overflow. Amen. That day you needed Him to go before you to receive the results of a medical test; wasn't He there? Yes, He was! How often does our money flow come up short for this or that, but He provided just when you thought all possibilities were exhausted. So before thinking people should see who you are in Christ, know that only God sees and knows exactly where you are and what's going on! Trust me, God alone is enough.

Today I am grateful to my Savior for not giving up on me. He has afforded me this opportunity to free myself from all things that impede my progress of moving forward. I remember being afraid and saddened by the thought of telling my story. Thank you to those who have loved me even though you haven't always understood me.

CHAPTER 18

Finding My Purpose

God is love. Now, after all, I've done in my past, the disobedience, selfish indulgence, neglect, and abuse to myself and others, God has had so much mercy and, most importantly, His love for me is unconditional. God decided to make me His own before I was conceived, and I'm persuaded above all else now that I was in God and he alone placed me in a family where He wanted me to be.

I was taught and learned the principles that gave me reverence for him. God also knew that I would stray but kept a close watch over me until His appointed time when He would call me out of that dark wilderness and into His marvelous light. The Lord took care of everything that belonged to me as well, my children and family.

God is efficient. My heavenly Father placed me into a church with a body of believers where I would learn more about Him, study His word, and what was and is required of me as His child. The love God's people showed me changed my life and my perspectives. I now recognize His voice and experience intimacy with the Savior in daily prayer. l have always believed that I was chosen to be different, go through difficulties, be saved, and have an opportunity to repent. Chosen to share love and to suffer for the sake of others, but not at all to the extent of Jesus, only what I could bare.

Please remember that no matter the crisis, obstacle, or situation, it's always easier having Jesus Christ as your constant companion!

God has been patient. I was given room and time to grow from who I was to who I am today. My growing pains at times felt detrimental. However, I soon learned and observed that God was always with me, leading and guiding me through. The comfort of knowing He was there and would never leave me to do what I needed to do alone was my greatest joy. Another great thing that happened while He patiently waited for me was that I began to feel confident about living my new life.

CHAPTER 19

Into The Light

arlier in my story, I shared that, while in prison, I worked in an optical lab servicing many prisons around the country with eyeglasses. My affiliation with the company aided me in finding and securing employment. Exactly one year later, after I decided to obey God's command to become celibate (December 7, 1991), I was personally invited to the Governor's Mansion by then Governor, Lawton Chiles, and the CEO of Pride of Florida, Pamela Jo Davis, on December 7, 1992. The recognition was to encourage and inspire rehabilitation.

God has kept right on doing great things for my family and me.

I've been on my Christian journey for thirty-four years and counting. My life has literally been moving from glory to glory! For thirty-two years since my release, I've been employed using skills taught while incarcerated. This program trained me and also enabled me to expand my education.

Late in 1993, I received a call from Mr. Tim Mann, representing Pride of Florida, expressing how proud the organization was of my accomplishments and that he would like to do more for me. He went on to ask me if I had ever considered going back to school. I answered, "Yes, I have." He told me that if I committed to completion, the Pride of Florida would pay for everything I needed a loan for.

I couldn't believe what I was hearing. All I know is that the Lord will give you the desires of your heart when you've given Him your life. No one knew that I wanted to attend school. I desperately needed to prove to myself that all wasn't lost. Upon my release, I became so busy with work, catching busses and spending time with my children that the desire for school was pushed back so far that I never had the time to pursue it. Only God!

I started my studies on February 14, 1994, and graduated on September 13, 1996, with an associate degree in Business Management. Pride also invited me to speak at one of their Management Council meetings held in Ocala, Florida. This purpose was to encourage the leaders that their efforts were not in vain.

As I think of where God brought me from and all that He has done and is doing in my life, I'm sure that one of the most precious gifts given to me was my Pastor Eric H. Jones, Jr. I believe that God saved and prepared this place of safety with me in His heart and mind. I've been to many places, and I would not have made this journey without the teachings I have received the leadership of this good shepherd.

I will forever praise God for the sacrifice and service of those who prayed with me, cried with me, and supported me when I needed it. There are many with this testimony, but today I'm privileged to share what a blessing to have the gift of a great teacher.

Pictured from left to right: Pamela Jo Davis, President of Pride, Shirley Hodges, my sister, Pamela Gillins (me), Governor Lawton Chiles

Prospect Hall

Hollywood, Florida

Under the standards of the Accrediting Commission of the Association of Independent Colleges and Schools, by Authority of the Board of Directors, and upon the recommendation of the Faculty

Pamela Patricia Fillins

has satisfactorily completed the program of studies for

Computer Business Administration and Management

and is awarded this

Specialized Associate Degree

with all the Honors and Privileges thereto appertaining.

In Witness Whereof, we have hereunto affixed our signatures

This Friday Thirteenth of September Nineteen Hundred and Ninety Six.

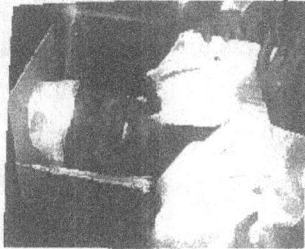

President

George W. Anderson
Dean of Academics

Registrar

CHAPTER 20

Finding A Home Within The Body

God Bless Eric and Bloneva Jones! I had the privilege of serving with the Sunday school ministry for seventeen years while also serving as a facilitator in a women's ministry, Singleness. My mentors encouraged and taught me how to share life's lessons that the Lord was teaching me about living and staying in His will as a single woman. I'm grateful that God proved His word to me: "Greater is He that is in me than he that is in the world."

Yes, our God has made all things work together for my good!

I have thirty-one years of abstinence from sex in celibacy. This was possible because I kept my promise to obey His word once I understood what was required of me. I know this is only one area; however, the sin of fornication cuts off communication and closes many doors that would otherwise be opened to you. Not to mention that your value to other men goes way down.

Today I can honestly say that I have truly lost nothing. I have gained so much that it's impossible to name it all, but here are a few important areas where God restored me: I have gained the love of family, which I missed terribly, and gained self-worth. I am a precious jewel and have gained self-confidence knowing that I can do all things through Christ, who gives me strength, self-love, and seeing myself as God sees me. My most guarded gift is that, as wretched as I was, I still have the awesome privilege of experiencing the greatest love of all, that God loved me so much that He sent His Son to die so that I and others may live again with Him. No Greater Gift Ever!

CHAPTER 21

Overlooked By Man, Handpicked By God

"For the Lord seeth not as man seeth."

1 SAMUEL 16:4, KJV

What I thought were some of my life's worst situations were not as bad as some things I experienced after salvation. During the restoration of and in my life, I became a target of the enemy. He used every scheme he had in his bag of tricks to discourage me and turn me back to the old way I lived. It didn't happen this time. Too late, I surrendered my life to the master. All praises to God.

The Lord promised me that He would bring my three children back to me. He did just what He said He would. Amen.

Knowing the mountain of a mess I made, I felt my circumstances were beyond saving. But God, yes, He began increasing my faith daily by allowing me to experience blessings in areas of my life that no one could have imagined or asked for. Now I realize and understand that all things are possible with God.

Let me explain. My daughter was sixteen with one son and another on the way. She went through her phase of, "You didn't love me; you're not my mother." I never responded to her verbally because I wasn't sure what to say. However, I was led to move out of my sister's home but kept the lines of communication open. I needed her to express all she felt due to my leaving her with my sister.

Also, I wanted to be very careful not to get in God's way. I knew that He did not need my help.

My son was cared for by the same sister since he was six months old. He was truly her baby. At eleven, I could never just walk in and take either of them from her. Cynthia loved both children as her very own. One day my son got into trouble in school and needed to go to court. My sister asked me to take him, and I did. Once there, the judge decided that my son needed an alternative school. The school the court chose was only two blocks from where I lived. There was no other way for him to attend school, so he had no choice but to live with me. My first child was returned to me at this time, and my confidence and faith were at an all-time high.

After all my disobedience, selfish indulgence, and rebellion, the Lord still had mercy on me. The Lord's love protected me. His predestination placed me into the family of His choice, where I would learn to reverence and respect the laws and powers that be. He (God) knew that I would stray but kept a close watch over me until the time came when He would call me out of the dark wilderness and into His marvelous light. Calling me out was great, but the gift that my calling was wrapped in was my pastor and the body of believers that instructed me in righteousness. Every teacher was committed to teaching us how to glorify God's way. My mentors and believers cared for me with lots of love and patience as a newborn baby as I truly was.

I was taught what is required of me as a steward. I'm still learning and have obtained intimacy through prayer and study. The Word has prepared me for the troubled waters I needed to go through without losing my testimony.

When praising and giving thanks, I feel like my Spirit leaps and raises me off the ground. Who would have thought I would have gotten to know the Lord as I do? Wow. I've experienced God's gift for over thirty years, but God has not received mine. Isn't this the true meaning of salvation? God wants His glory to be seen so that others will believe and come to Him. Our testimony should showcase the majestic and awesome power of the miracles performed in our lives.

It doesn't matter how low you have bowed to this world; He alone can make something beautiful and good out of your life. You are not what you do or have done. You are not what you wear or drive. You are not what people say about you or even what your own mind tells you about yourself. We are who God says we are, wonderfully made by Him. (See Psalm 139)

Our great creator has poured Himself into every living being. Everything about Jehovah is great. So, my sister and brother, what has been placed inside you is a greatness that may be hidden for a time; however, when the Lord is ready to show His abundant mercy and grace, He will inspire you from within. So prepare yourself by reading the Word, activate your prayer life, and listen to the leading of the Holy Spirit, who will guide you to places you never believed possible for you. And then, behold, you will begin to really see yourself. You will see the masterpiece that the Lord has made, You!

As we journey with God and move and serve in areas within the church's walls, we discover that some people may never agree that there are no little me and big you. Amen.

Let me share one thing that happened to me, and I'm sure I have not been the only one to experience this. I pray that if this has happened to others, their concerns and hurt are taken to the one who matters the most and can make it beautiful.

I served faithfully in ministry for seventeen years and thought that fellowship was restored among my sisters and brothers. After a few years in ministry, I noticed that I was never invited to the end-of-the-year celebration that the pastor would give in appreciation for the sacrifice and faithfulness of the volunteers. At first, I tried to ignore it, but I never made the list year after year. Around my fifteenth year, the feeling of being overlooked and the thoughts that my service wasn't meaningful enough almost caused me to stumble. Instead of remembering who I was serving, God, not man. That human part of me felt my sacrifice didn't matter to people. I must admit that I spent time thinking of why I wasn't in attendance. After a while, the Lord assured me that He had never left me out of anything. Each time blessings were passed out, my name was on His list. Amen.

I have a friend who would come to my home often during this time. The friend worked at the church and even participated in the planning of several events. At one point, in my distress about being overlooked, I felt my friend was a part of this mess that flooded my mind. I thank God He always stops us in our tracks, allowing us to dismiss negative delusions from the enemy. My friend and I were spiritually in similar places when we met over thirty years ago, and because of this, I sometimes pulled away from her so as not to do or say anything that would damage our friendship. I know she felt my drifting, but I sensed that it was better to allow the Counselor within to counsel me on what was happening. I know very well the terrible way the old woman handled situations. I've learned that when you care for someone, you will always consider their feelings. So I tried really hard to understand why. The Holy Spirit, my Counselor within, needed to work overtime to help me with this type of rejection. Sisters and brothers, I was wrong. I didn't need to be in those rooms.

Today I understand that I was not overlooked. God chose the path for me to take. The Lord knew I needed more personal prayer and study time to prepare for what and where He was leading me.

I truly thank the Lord, who has privileged me to be free. Free from what the enemy's weapon of spiritual warfare could have caused. I believe the weapon was designed to rob me of all the growth and maturity the Lord has given me. I will continue to pray for the individual who might pick up and leave a good Bible-teaching church with a pastor who loves God's people and allows all to grow gracefully. When I say I love you, it comes from a pure heart, knowing that I mess up and fall short too, and will continue to press toward perfection. I will always forgive because I'm standing as forgiven. Yes, I finally understand.

CHAPTER 22

Something Beautiful, Something Good

The testimony of my early years teaches us just how early the adversary attempts to destroy the purpose God has ordained for a person's life. Psalm 139 says God knit me together from the very beginning in my mother's womb. I have been fearfully and wonderfully made. Verse 16 from the same chapter says, "Your eyes saw my unformed body; all the days ordained for me were written in your book before one of them came to be." Psalm 139:16 (NIV)

Understanding the word of the Lord now gives me confidence and assurance that He was with me every step of the way. I am free from my past because it was in my future from the beginning. Amen!

From the start, the love in my heart was sufficient to stand me up in the face of doubt and the belief that NO ONE cared or loved me. That love kept me in the battle for restoration.

I have said to my pastor, Dr. Eric H. Jones Jr., when the Lord called him to preach to lost souls, He (God) had me in mind. The word and teaching from Dr. Jones' sermons were exactly what God knew I needed. The pastor preached and confirmed God's words in my private time alone with Him.

Remember when I agreed to attend the Watch Night service, I sat on the last row near the door to have easy access to the exit. That night I immediately knew that was the place I needed to be.

Through the years, I've encountered folks that remember things that I did, but for some reason, I see very pleasant amazement in their eyes. I have almost always been able to attribute my new life to Jesus Christ.

While in prison, we would sing the song Something Beautiful, Something Good. Out of all my confusion, He understood. All I had to offer was brokenness and strife, but He made something beautiful of my life. Then one Sunday, my pastor's wife began to sing that very song that touched my heart when I was still in bondage. She sang with so much passion and encouragement that these words will always be a part of my testimony.

I believe them for you too. Are you ready to allow God to make something beautiful and something good out of your life? Why not start today? Ask the Savior to come into your heart. Believe that Jesus was born and that He died for your sins. Believe today that He has promised you everlasting life because God raised Jesus from the dead. Your life will never be the same if you truly believe!

Acknowledgments

Jesus Christ who chose me.

"You have not chosen me, but I have chosen you and ordained you, that you should go and bring forth fruit, and that your fruit shall remain, that whatsoever you shall ask of the father in my name, He may give it to you."

JOHN 15:16

To my dear sister Cynthia, who cared for my two children as if she had given birth to them herself! I thanked her for her sacrifice while she was with us; now, she has received her crown. To my sisters, Shirley and Nora, these two acknowledged the gift of God in me, believing my transformation was real. They are not with us today, but by faith, I believe their prayers helped me complete this task. To my sister Ruby, thank you for reassuring me at the beginning that the LORD promised to save me. You were not surprised when I called you so excited about my conversion. All you said was, "God told me He would." My praying sisters, I praise God for your fellowship and genuine love for my family and me.

To my church family, thank you for allowing me to grow in your presence and under your guidance. Thank you for praying for our family when I could not go on. When I say I love you, I am speaking from my heart.

To my prayer partner, Diane Smith, no words can express your love and how you never changed your position where my family or I were concerned. You have remained my friend even when I wavered. Keep holding up the banner of hope for us all. Thanks.

To the PRIDE of Florida, Mr. Gudhaus, thank you for believing in me and supporting me. Advantage Optics, Premium Optics, and the Scherer Family-God bless you for your continued support down through the years. I appreciate you all.

To my brother, Chip, who has always supported me with whatever and whenever it was needed, I love you.

To my nephew, Michiah and Renada, thank you so very much for giving me the space to do all that was needed to accomplish this 'Great Thing' God gave me to do. Your love and patience have been paramount.

My prayer partners, my godmother Irene Rufus, Vickie Butler, Helena Stephens, and my dear Sister Diane Smith, I praise God for you all being in my life.

Finally, to my children, Antoinette, Ronald and Calvin thank you for your love and respect down through the years. I have loved you from your beginnings.

To my grandchildren, Trenton, Ferris Jr., and Shanyah. You have been a blessing from God and thank you for letting me love you. We are living in the promises of the Lord! Don't ever forget the One who has the power to give life also has the power to take it away! Seek the Lord while He may be found.

In Jesus Name.

Speaking Engagements

Pamela is passionate about God's mandate to seek and save the lost and to set the captives free.

To request Pamela for a speaking engagement, book signing, prison ministry or to speak at your church event, please contact Pamela at _Ppgillins60@icloud.com_.